A CHOIR FOR ALL

A behind-the-scenes record of Trinity Boys Choir

written and photographed by

ROGER MAILE ARPS

A CHOIR FOR ALL SEASONS
by Roger Maile
Published by Creative Monochrome
20 St Peters Road, Croydon, Surrey, CR0 1HD.

© Roger Maile, November 1990.
ISBN 1 873319 00 2
First edition, 1990.

Fairies
Glyndebourne tour, 1985

One of several generations of fairies for Benjamin Britten's opera, *A Midsummer Night's Dream.* TBC has fulfilled this role in three very different professional productions.

Preface

My first experience of Trinity Boys Choir came in 1972 at Fairfield Halls in Croydon, shortly before I took up office as Headmaster. To experience a packed house in a major concert hall, and a performance of two children's operas, one of them Britten's *Golden Vanity* (for which no critical concessions were needed for their being the work of a school), told me clearly that I was to be involved with a remarkable enterprise.

Eighteen years later, I still find it remarkable that perfectly ordinary schoolboys, some of whom probably did not even think that they could sing, can year after year be brought to such a high standard that a constant stream of invitations arrive to work in a variety of professional milieus. Some are glamorous, such as the generations of 'fairies' sent to Glyndebourne, Aldeburgh and the Royal Opera House; some may seem trivial, such as advertising jingles; some are amusing, such as singing deliberately badly for a *Monty Python* album. All invitations are judged by the same criteria: will the experience enhance the boys' education, and will any consequent absences from school be justified?

This splendid collection of photographs will evoke many memories for the followers of Trinity Boys Choir. For those to whom it is an introduction, let me stress that these achievements do not come from a specialised music school. Music is but one of the many activities pursued vigorously as an important element of the boys' general education. Indeed, most of last season's pack in the very successful Rugby XV were also members of Trinity Choristers. So it should be.

Robin Wilson
Headmaster
Trinity School, Croydon

October 1990

Another 'Dream'
Royal Opera House, Covent Garden, 1986

The Covent Garden production of *A Midsummer Night's Dream*
made great demands on the boys' acting and movement abilities in
addition to their singing skills. The photograph shows the boys
during a break in their vocal warm-up in a rehearsal room high
above the auditorium.

Contents

Procession
Limpsfield Parish Church, 1981

One of the moody, misty shots taken during the filming of the TV advertisement for the *Ronco* record, *Count Your Blessings* – the assignment which started this 10-year photographic project.

1 *That Ronco photo*

This book is a personal photographic record. It sets out to give a flavour of what goes into making Trinity Boys Choir one of the most accomplished in the country. It is, if you like, a record of the private life behind the public performance.

It all started about ten years ago. I was then working as a teacher at Trinity School, an independent day school for boys on the outskirts of Croydon. Although my chief academic responsibility was exposing the sixth form to the mysterious world of economics, the ethos of the school was (and, indeed, still is) geared to staff taking a wide involvement in a whole range of extra-curricular activities.

As a keen photographer from youth, it was natural that one of the areas I became involved in was taking photographs of a variety of events, from school plays and rugby matches to team photos and VIP guests. Most of these creative gems went no further than the school magazine or prospectus, although several later turned up in my Associateship portfolio for the Royal Photographic Society. Having gained the ARPS, I left the school around six years ago to turn 'pro'. But, as it turned out, that was far from the end of my photographic involvement with Trinity.

The primary responsibility for my continuing interest in the school, and hence this book, sits squarely on the shoulders of David Squibb, Trinity's Director of Music.

Being unable to play any musical instrument, incapable of singing a note in tune, and having an interest in music that started with *The Beatles* and continued in similar vein, I had apparently little in common with David. We were, however, brought into a primitive form of professional relationship through the geography of the school. On joining Trinity, my classroom was a temporary building (fondly, but not entirely appropriately, referred to as 'the hut') which had been implanted outside David's sanctum, the Music Room. Consequently, as I stood at my blackboard, I often found myself an involuntary spectator of David's classes.

'Spectator' is not really the right word. One hears music. I certainly heard it, as did my classes. David's gramophone – I'm sure he would never have called it a 'record player' – was conveniently placed close to a usually opened window, and provided a sometimes welcome accompaniment to the dismal science. Never welcome, however, was the time of year when rehearsals began for the ritual junior music competition.

The impossible takes a little longer

Limpsfield Parish Church, 1981

For the *Ronco* advert, the boys had to process into the harsh
October sunlight: looking angelic, singing, walking in line, not
looking down or at the camera, and not protecting their eyes from
the glare of the sun. It takes time, but it can be – and was – done.

The discordant – even to my untrained ear – noise was a less than subtle form of torture to which my classes usually responded by wincing, howling like tormented wolves or dissolving into uncontrollable hysteria.

But the interaction between the two classrooms extended beyond this annual cacophony. One of the strange things about teaching is that you do not usually see your colleagues in performance. Whether intentional or not, David and I were often guilty of breaking this taboo. He might look up to see me conducting his recorded overture or, in the middle of one of my Basil Fawlty rages, I might suddenly become aware of one more bemused spectator than I had expected. The more bizarre activities in our

respective provinces sometimes occasioned a break-time explanation, and the seeds of a lengthy friendship were sown.

One of the many skills which David brings to his role as Director of Music is the ability to 'motivate' boys, parents and staff to support and participate in the musical achievements of the School. Thus, it should have been no surprise when David persuaded me to take some photographs for the Trinity Boys Choir (TBC). That was ten years ago.

Although being sufficiently naïve to be flattered by his request, I freely admit to having been less than excited by the prospect. The 'assignment' was to cover a video recording at a local church for a

Facing the cameras
Ronco *record TV advertisement, 1981*

A break between 'takes' during the filming of the advertisement for the *Ronco* Christmas record, *Count Your Blessings*, in the grounds of Limpsfield Parish Church. A hard day's work to produce a 30-second commercial.

television advertisement to promote a Christmas album the Choir had recorded for *Ronco*. David wanted some still shots that he could use for the Choir's publicity purposes.

Most of the photographs I took on the appointed day, I am almost ashamed to admit, were conventional groups of the angelic host. This, I assumed, was what was wanted. In true Christmas card tradition, these shots were replete with candlelit starbursts, misted filters and angelic faces. Very nice too, if you like that sort of thing, but nothing that hasn't been done countless times before.

One of the shots the video director had planned for the advertisement was a candlelit procession, the boys innocent in their choir robes, from the choir stalls to the aisle of the church. It proved a very difficult shot to get right. It was hard, for a start, to get a camera angle where the boys were not inadvertently masking one another. Then there was the usual range of problems: the boys were either not looking sufficiently angelic or were moving at the wrong speed; the candles would flicker out; tape, lights or sound would fail; and so the catalogue of problems continued.

Time after time, under the heat of the video lighting and weight of their choir robes, the boys made their slow procession down the aisle. After the 'cut' at the end of each take, the boys waited patiently as the director crouched over a small monitor to review the film.

Repeatedly, one small imperfection (or, indeed, the hope that an even better

'take' was possible) would occasion a repeat performance.

After what must have been fourteen attempts, the director called 'cut' yet again and returned to the video playback on his monitor. As their faces portrayed their tiredness and frustration, the boys turned towards the monitor to witness their latest effort in the hope that the director would, at last, be satisfied. That 'golden moment' arrived and, for once, the camera captured in that split second the full story of the day's events etched in those pitiful expressions. It was this shot which later became known between

Every mother's son
Limpsfield Parish Church, 1981

Candlelit procession
Limpsfield Parish Church, 1981

The filming of the much-repeated candlelit procession for the
Ronco advertisement.

David and me, quite simply, as 'That Ronco Photo'.

Some days after the event, I visited David to run through the proofs from the day's work. As he perused the 'picture postcard' prints, David was making very generous comments and showing considerable appreciation of the results.

It has often been my experience that what the photographer likes does not coincide with the client's preferences. A shot of a child picking his nose may make a more amusing photograph than the normal school portrait, but it is not what most doting mums want to display on the mantelpiece. With this in mind, I am usually quite careful about putting proofs in order: starting with the ones the client expects, in ascending order of merit, then ending with one or two shots that I particularly like. The theory – if that is not too elevated a description – is that the first few prints set the level of expectation, which is exceeded by the shots that follow, so that any 'oddball' photos at the end have a better chance of receiving a favourable response.

This was exactly the technique I used with the proofs I was showing David. (Indeed, I still do, although this printed revelation may necessitate a change of practice in future.) As he progressed through the pile, all was going to plan: he was showing increasing signs of satisfaction. All the time, the thought was going through my mind that I should not have risked including, as the last print, 'That Ronco Photo' of those tired expressions.

There were several reasons supporting my doubt. The most damning indictment any schoolboy can make of an activity is that "it's boring" – a phrase not generally used sparingly by the species. As I thought that David might want to use such photographs to attract boys into the Choir, a group shot showing what appeared to be boredom beyond belief was hardly likely to meet his needs. Moreover, there was the danger that this aberration might detract from the rest of my work or even be taken as some sort of intended insult.

The moment came when David turned to the last print. I could feel my face reddening. There was a pause as he took in the subject matter. Then he burst out laughing.

From the discussion that followed, it became apparent that this was exactly the sort of candid photograph David was looking for. He could appreciate the value of formal, staged shots, but these are generally quite readily available from the sponsors or organisers of events. What David really wanted was a more informal view – something that would give a fuller impression of what the life of the Choir is really like.

We were in business. This was exactly the sort of photograph that I would find interesting and enjoyable to take. It is ironic now to look back on 'That Ronco Photo' – and particularly my misgivings about showing it to David – and to think of the many enjoyable days and nights of challenging photography in some of the best known public venues in the country which it led to.

'That Ronco Photo'
Limpsfield Parish Church, 1981

The photograph which, for me, encapsulated the trials of the long day's filming and which, much to my surprise, led to a 10-year project photographing Trinity Boys Choir in a variety of prestigious venues.

This book is not the culmination of my sojourn with the Choir which 'That Ronco Photo' initiated – it is a progress report. The combination of a new decade, the 10th anniversary of my involvement, and the 25th anniversary of the Choir itself, seemed like a good time to present such a report.

The promise of that first assignment has been fulfilled by subsequent events. During the past 10 years, I have been able to photograph the Choir in several Glyndebourne performances, at the Royal Opera House, Covent Garden, at the Aldeburgh Festival, and at the Royal Albert Hall and the Barbican, amongst many other venues. I am grateful to the management and press officers of these venues and to the producers and organisers of the events – too many to mention individually – for the co-operation they have shown me. I have been privileged to wander back stage, to attend rehearsals, to photograph on stage, following the boys as their work in each production progressed towards the public performance.

Whilst the photographs will, I hope, be of interest in themselves, they are not generally self-explanatory; so I have added a brief commentary to place the photographs in the context of the events. I have also included some background about the Choir and its work, including David Squibb's perspective and the views of some of the boys who are currently members of the Choir.

If the photographs in this book succeed in conveying the spontaneity, fun, enthusiasm and endeavour of the Choir, it is due entirely to the professionalism of the boys. They have allowed me to point my lenses in their direction, often in the confines of cramped dressing rooms in the tense moments before a major performance, without playing to the camera or any hint of irritation. They haven't even been safe from the camera when travelling, eating or finding a quiet place to finish their homework. They have co-operated, without objection, with photo-calls, extra rehearsals and publicity shots.

I hope that when they see this book, they will feel it has all been worthwhile and that it forms an interesting record and a fitting tribute to their many achievements over the years.

2   *A part of real life*

Trinity Boys Choir is remarkable for a number of reasons, not least of which is the number and range of professional music assignments it has undertaken. The Choir's work spans the musical spectrum from classical opera and recitals of religious music to film soundtracks and contemporary popular music recordings. The venues performed in range from cathedrals to village churches and from the Palace Theatre, Manchester to London clubs.

My photographic sojourn with the Choir is both short, by comparison with its 25-year history, and far from comprehensive, even in its coverage of the last 10 years. If this were not so, I would be able to show photographs in this book to give even stronger evidence of TBC's versatility.

For example, I regret missing the opportunity to photograph the two solo boys perched in the dizzy heights of the Royal Albert Hall in Henze's large-scale and dissonant *Raft of the Medusa*. Then there was the performance of Britten's *War Requiem* in the open-air Herodius Atticus in Athens. The shots that got away also include the boys appearing with Bing Crosby in his last Christmas TV show and Leonard Bernstein supporting a fainting Trinity boy during the rehearsal for the Stravinsky *Mass*.

In more sadistic moments, I also regret that I was not behind the camera when the boys performed in an open-air concert in Holland Park during a severe thunderstorm, or when they were stranded overnight at a London airport hotel.

These 'if only' examples serve to underline the range of work the Choir has been involved in over the years, and the level of success it has attained. It really is, as this book's title says, *A choir for all seasons*.

The TBC story is all the more remarkable given the nature of the school. Trinity is neither a specialist music school nor a boarding school. Entrance is competitive, on the basis of academic potential; there are some instrumental scholarships, but candidates have to meet the academic criteria as well as show musical aptitude. And the Choir is just one of a large number of extra-curricular activities vying for the boys' time on a voluntary basis. In this context, to be able regularly to field choirs of anything from 10 to 100 boys performing to the highest professional standards is quite exceptional.

At the centre of this achievement, and very much its driving force, is David Squibb, the School's Director of Music. The last person who would want me to

David Squibb, Director of Music

Conducting the Choir at Fairfield Hall, Croydon, 1982

David Squibb founded Trinity Boys Choir soon after he joined the teaching staff at the School in 1964. Typical of his attitude was his amused reaction to this photograph: "I don't know why you bothered to take that – people want to see the boys, not me."

say this is David himself. He is a modest man, who believes strongly in teamwork and has an almost obsessive dislike of the cult of the individual. There are no stars in the Choir – so much so that it was quite a job even to get him to agree to me naming some of the individual boys featured in the photographs in this book. David is the first person to credit the boys for the Choir's achievements and to point to the vital role in its success played by his teaching colleagues (and indeed his wife, Shirley).

We have spent many a train journey to and from Glyndebourne discussing the Choir's work, how it fits into the boys' overall education, the antics of individual boys, and the attitude of parents, fellow teachers and the school management. Underlining his infectious enthusiasm and total commitment to his work is a ready wit and engaging generosity of spirit.

From the time he arrived at Trinity in 1964, David's ambition has been to involve as many boys as possible in a diversity of musical activities, whilst achieving a consistently high standard of performance.

He sees public performance as a vital part of musical activity: "If sports teams go and play games outside the school, then why not musicians? If the rugby players or any other sports teams were just confined to playing against each other in school, they would get bored. The real fun is in going outside and playing teams they don't know – seeing how their skills match up. I believe it's much the same with music. It makes

music a part of real life, rather than just a school subject."

Getting the opportunity to perform on the public stage is another matter. In the early days, it started with church even-songs and local choral societies. David's connections with the BBC – he had freelanced as a music journalist for some years before joining Trinity – brought an early radio broadcast.

This is not the place for a detailed history of the Trinity Boys Choir. Suffice it to say that perhaps the big break was the invitation to perform in the lunchtime concert series at Fairfield Hall, Croydon, usually reserved for more established professional soloists. The performance of Britten's *Missa Brevis* and *Golden Vanity* went well and led to further invitations, including the sell-out performance of Richard Rodney Bennett's children's opera, *All the King's Men* and subsequent regular evening concert dates at Fairfield. When *All the King's Men* was taken successfully to London in tandem with the premiere of Edmund Rubbra's *Missa Brevis,* commissioned by Trinity School, the Choir's national reputation was in the making. A record and Granada television production of *All the King's Men* soon followed, along with a host of other enviable and diverse professional opportunities.

"I was interested in children's operas from the start," says David Squibb. "It means you can involve large numbers of boys and can give them the opportunity to really let themselves go. It's a valuable educational experience and I have found that it actually helps

Christmas concert
Fairfield Hall, 1982

Trinity's connection with the lunchtime concert series at Fairfield
Hall, Croydon, goes back to the early days of the Choir. The annual
Christmas concert has become an established favourite in
the venue's seasonal programme.

Music for all

Rehearsal at Trinity School for the children's opera, Bang!*, 1982*

John Rutter's *Bang!* – based on the gunpowder plot – was commissioned by the School and has been staged on several occasions at Fairfield Hall, Croydon. The premiere in this 1550-seat concert hall was fully booked weeks in advance.

their musicianship and greatly improves their versatility."

In what is a very competitive South London market for quality public day schools, there is no doubt that Trinity's music reputation is a distinct attraction to some boys and their parents. This was summed up nicely for me by a friend whose son was about to take the entrance examination: "I want him to go to a school where no-one thinks you're odd if you turn up carrying a violin case." At Trinity, the boy is likely to have his sports bag in the other hand.

"Music is not an exclusive activity," David Squibb is keen to emphasise. "I firmly believe that the boys miss out if they don't participate in other things."

The boys in TBC clearly gain a great deal from the experience. "Obviously public performance sets a definite goal and brings a sense of achievement," says David Squibb. "It also helps the development of their self confidence and awareness. The range of activities they are involved in means that they have to be well organised. They tend to become good at making decisions, dealing with important things first and thinking quickly. It's hard work, but above all, it has to be fun."

David has a great deal of respect for the boys' work, although he is noted for being sparing in his praise: "I feel privileged to be part of seeing them achieve certain things. Sometimes it can be quite moving. I particularly remember our first production at the Aldeburgh Festival. We were staying in a marvellous house right next to the sea, during a wonderful summer, and performing in an excellent production of *The Dream* in the superb setting of 'The Maltings' at Snape. I remember thinking what a lucky bloke I am to be part of all this. The next minute, of course, the boys were shrieking and beating each other up, and it was back to reality."

3   *Trinity Choristers*

The formation of Trinity Choristers in 1965, when the School moved to its current site from the centre of Croydon, is really the start of the Trinity Boys Choir story. David Squibb was aware that several boys sang in local church choirs, while others were in the Royal School of Church Music, at nearby Addington Palace. It seemed ridiculous not to acknowledge this within Trinity, and so he hit upon the idea of forming the school's own full harmony church choir, with upper and lower voices – probably unique within the country for a day school without a chapel.

The idea supported David's ambition to take music outside the school. The first 'performance' was evensong at Maidstone Parish Church, since when the Choristers have sung services and recitals in churches and cathedrals throughout the length and breadth of the country. To this day, membership of

Evensong
St Peter's Church, Croydon, 1989

Trinity Choristers is the School's church choir, which sings services and recitals of religious music at different churches and cathedrals throughout the country – supporting the objective of taking the boys' music out into the community.

Sweet singing in the choir
Evensong at St Peter's Church, Croydon, 1989

the Choristers is restricted to those boys who are either members of a church choir or, occasionally, regular attenders of churches without a choir. Trinity Boys Choir, on the other hand, is open to all boys in the school who have the singing potential. The Choristers is the only 'permanent' group within TBC – in other cases, a new choir is selected for each event. Forming new groups provides the opportunity to mix levels of experience, match abilities to the demands of the work, and develop new talent.

One of the original purposes of forming the Choristers was to support the sterling work of individual church choirs – the backbone of the choral music tradition in this country. Numerous choirmasters have commented on how the additional experience the boys gain in Trinity Choristers also benefits their local church choirs.

The high point of the Trinity Choristers year is the annual residential course at a cathedral. In 1969, when the courses first started, the idea of a guest boys' choir singing services while the cathedral choir was on holiday was something of a novelty. There is more competition now, of varying standards, but Trinity Choristers have found a welcome every year since 1969, visiting some 20 different cathedrals.

The courses usually last around 10 days. David Squibb sums up their significance:

"It's a very concentrated period of intense effort. We deliberately put on demanding programmes, not just in the cathedral, but also at churches in the locality. Many of the pieces have to be learnt on the course: there isn't time to prepare every work in advance. It is the major opportunity each year to raise the whole standard of the boys' work – things like sight reading improve dramatically, for example. But just as they work hard, so they play hard – there's always plenty of opportunity to let off steam.

"It's a very valuable experience to work in wonderful buildings and to get an insight into the life of a cathedral choir. There's a tremendous responsibility thrown on them because they're in the public eye for much of the time. And, of course, for many of them it's their first time away from home without their parents. There are the occasional cases of being homesick, but there's so much going on that these don't usually last long.

"By the end of the course they have achieved so much – on so many different levels – that it gives a real boost to their self confidence. It's something they remember for a long time. Whenever I meet past members of the Choristers, the conversation inevitably turns to one of the cathedral courses, often a vividly detailed recollection of an incident that had quite slipped my memory."

(Both photographs)
Religious recital
*Church of St Michael and
All Angels, Croydon, 1990*

A local recital of some of
the religious music in the
repertoire from the
Worcester Cathedral
residential course.

Choristers
*St Peter's Church,
Croydon, 1989*

There is a natural
tendency for people to
behave unnaturally when a
camera is pointed at them.
With the Choristers,
however, the demands of
concentrating on the music
and the conducting of the
choirmaster help to
overcome this tendency. I
also find, as this series of
photographs shows, that
keeping my camera in the
same direction for some
period of time helps the
boys to forget I'm there.

4   *It's not just singing*

The public performance is the tip of the musical iceberg. What goes on behind the scenes to make the performance possible and to achieve such high standards is a story in itself. This is particularly true of the many professional opera productions the Choir has been involved in.

Operas represent a special challenge to the boys, making demands not just on their singing skills, but involving make-up, costumes, learning their parts, and movement/dance and acting ability. At the same time, they have to keep up with school work and fit in all their other activities.

Typically, an opera production will start with auditions. The chosen boys face a concentrated series of rehearsals, initially in school, for both the singing and sometimes the acting elements of their roles. Nearer the event, they will join with the rest of the cast either at the venue itself or in a rehearsal studio, starting to learn the required stage positions and movements and the

(Left)
Elizabethan fairy
Glyndebourne production of The Dream, *1989*

Getting used to working in elaborate costumes, wigs and make-up is just one aspect of the challenge operas present.

(Right)
***Bang!* rehearsal**
Trinity School, 1982

Any production requires many rehearsals before it is ready for public performance. Here, the boys practice animated conversation for one of the crowd scenes.

Vocal rehearsal

Glyndebourne, 1987

After a warm-up for the full choir in one of Glyndebourne's
rehearsal rooms, David Squibb gives additional tuition to two of
the younger singers.

interaction with other players. In the days preceding the first night, rehearsals become more intensive, and the boys have to start getting used to make-up and costumes.

"I often wonder whether I should be more serious in rehearsals," David Squibb confides. "We take the job seriously enough, but there's a lot of fun and silly banter along the way. I'm sure that on some occasions anyone watching our antics would wonder how we ever achieved anything."

The 1986 Royal Opera House production of Britten's *A Midsummer Night's Dream* required a particular emphasis on movement, working with director Christopher Renshaw and choreographer Terry Etheridge. David Squibb recalls the production with obvious relish: "It was a splendid example of how well things can go when the right people are in charge. They just expect the boys to be able to do it, and the boys respond to this very positively and intelligently.

"That production really took the boys out of themselves. It was a revelation to me to see them control their bodies in response to the music. It was quite clear that this helped their singing enormously. Several of the parents remarked to me after the production that they had noticed a distinct change in their sons' general awareness and self confidence. That's what I mean about the Choir being an important part of their general education."

Most recently, I had the opportunity to photograph David Meyer, the director of the 1990 Sadlers Wells production of *The Dream*, taking the boys through their first movement rehearsal. He sat down with them for 40 minutes, by which time he had heard their stage histories, explained his philosophy of the plot and how it would be interpreted, discussed the set, their costumes and make-up, and answered questions ranging from how much actors are paid to his own acting role in *Octopussy*.

As someone who had believed that 12 year-old boys are incapable of sitting quietly in one place for ten minutes, I found their rapt attention quite remarkable. Admittedly, the boys did seem more at home in the remaining hour, when they were asked to behave as if they had never lived in a civilised society and were practising throwing bamboo canes at one another.

One other aspect of the public performance which is rarely seen is what I call the 'David Squibb travelling roadshow'. Supervising a dozen or more excitable youngsters on and off trains, dealing with interminable questions, organising fleets of taxis, allocating beds in hotel rooms, making sure that homework is completed, taking orders for every conceivable variation of pizza with every possible combination of drink, and making sure that everyone gets to the right place in the theatre at the right time, is no enviable task.

Even more difficult is dealing with the same boys after the performance, exuberant with the 'buzz' that inevitably follows the curtain call. This is particularly so at Glyndebourne, where a

It's not just singing
The first movement rehearsal for the Sadlers Wells production of
The Dream, *1990*

The boys start thinking themselves into their parts in response to
the director's prompt: "Imagine you've been brought up in the wild
by animals – how would you move?"

A matter of trust

The Sadlers Wells production of The Dream, *1990*

Director David Meyer (background centre) lets the protogé fairies loose with bamboo canes. In this first movement rehearsal, he is building trust with – and between – the boys, whilst ensuring a fair measure of fun to maintain interest.

coach replete with singers and orchestral musicians anxious to catch the last train back to London, awaits. Scrubbing off make-up and changing back into school uniform might not seem a particularly demanding task in the light of their other achievements, but it is always the most frenetic activity of the day. The boys are traditionally the last on the coach, greeted by much good-natured jeering from their fellow professionals. They have not missed the train yet.

The most surprising thing to me is the way David Squibb thrives on this existence. He puts it down to his National Service days as an instructor in the Junior Wing of the Royal Marines School of Music: "I really think that having to keep up with their antics, set me up for life."

He is phlegmatic, but certainly not complacent, on the question of discipline. "Just because they're going around in public, they do not stop being schoolboys. They will get up to mischief – something would be wrong if they didn't. Their music discipline is always excellent, because they know they're expected to be professional. It's a job that has to be done well. But when the opportunity arises, they need to let off steam, and they can very easily go over the top. So you have to be careful. You need to be able to pull them up, but in a slightly lighthearted way. They always know where the line is."

One of David's devices for demarcating that line is a complex system of black marks, which are a constant source of interest and argument for the boys and a complete mystery to me. As I understand it, achieving a certain total results in a 'court martial' at which other members of the Choir set a suitable punishment for the miscreant.

Whatever David's system is, I can vouch as a privileged observer that it certainly does work.

On the road to Glyndebourne
1989

(Left)
On the road again

The boys take over a corner of East Croydon station prior to
departing for another Glyndebourne performance – this time,
it's *Carmen*.

(Above)
On the move

A typical blur of activity as the boys rush to catch the train at
East Croydon.

Above all, it has to be fun

East Croydon station, 1987

The boys show obvious interest in a variation on the frisbee which
David Squibb has bought for them to help while away the long
intervals between their rehearsal calls at Glyndebourne. When
off-stage during public performances, they have to keep out of sight
of the audience, but rehearsals and television recordings give them
ample opportunity to play in the extensive grounds.

On tour

(Above) Music is never far away
Two boys share the output from a personal stereo – the fashion at the time was *The Beastie Boys*.

(Above right) Passing the time away
The boys amuse themselves on the train journey.

(Right) Taxi
The Glyndebourne tour of *The Dream* reaches Southampton. At the station, David negotiates for a fleet of taxis to ferry the boys to the hotel.

Glyndebourne tour, Southampton, 1985

(Right)
Pied piper
Surrounded by a huddle of boys, David makes his way towards the unsuspecting hotel.

(Left)
Vying for position
Allocating places in hotel rooms so that everyone is happy proves a more complex task than might be expected.

(Right)
Home from home
The boys settle down in their allotted room. I am assured the boy to the right is adjusting a yo-yo on his fingers, rather than preparing a gesture for the camera. The feet to the extreme right are equally intriguing!

Cleaning up
Southampton tour,
1985

After the performance,
getting the heavy
make-up off takes a lot
of care and attention
to detail.

Waiting in the wings
Bang! *rehearsal,*
Fairfield Hall, 1982

The priest awaits his
entrance. The
combination of the
shadows of the actors
on stage, the crucifix-
like pose of the priest
and the dramatic
lighting makes this one
of my favourite
photographs.

5 Waiting in the wings

During the period I've been taking photographs of the Choir, I have spent a lot of time waiting in the wings or backstage before, during and after public performances. For me, there is always something quite electric about the atmosphere, but it would be hard to detect that from the reactions of the boys, who seem more concerned about getting their quota of Coca-Cola than the activity all around them.

Let me take you, albeit selectively, through a typical evening at Glyndebourne during the production of *Carmen* to share my recollections. I should explain that David and I have a standing arrangement that for each new event he tells the boys that I am there to take photographs for the School and that they should ignore me and my cameras. Generally, they do. Quite often, we will pick out a couple of boys who I will

All together now
Glyndebourne, 1989

David takes the boys through a vocal warm-up soon after arriving at Glyndebourne.

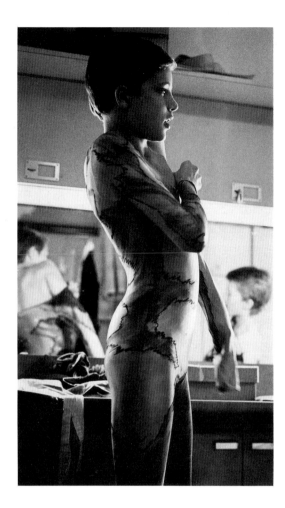

Changing
Royal Opera House, 1986

The tight body stockings worn by the fairies in the Covent Garden production of *The Dream* proved a struggle for growing boys.

follow closely throughout the day, so that I get the opportunity to photograph the full sequence of events.

The train trip to Lewes starts at East Croydon station in mid-afternoon. Sometimes this is an opportunity to catch up with homework, while others play cards, read, or amuse themselves in the sort of energetic conversation of which only schoolboys seem capable. Arriving at Lewes, a minibus awaits to hurtle us through the narrow Sussex lanes to rural Glyndebourne.

Being a musical philistine, I admit to having had no real preconception of what was so special about Glyndebourne before actually visiting it. I don't think I'd even heard of the traditional lengthy interval while the evening-dressed audience picnic in great style in the beautiful grounds. Subsequently, I've begun to understand why it is so highly prized by opera performers. What is readily apparent is the warm, family atmosphere, not just amongst the cast but throughout the team which it takes to bring an opera to fruition.

Arriving at Glyndebourne, David checks-in with 'the planning office' to confirm the arrangements for warm-up rooms. The boys navigate their way to the dressing rooms as if they had known the place from birth. Waiting to greet them like long lost sons is their 'dresser', fondly known as Tuppence (but that's another story). Tuppence has looked after several generations of Trinity boys at Glyndebourne and never has a bad word to say about them. After a territorial fight for favoured pegs and

Settling in
Glyndebourne tour,
Southampton, 1985

Waiting for the costumes
to arrive in the dressing
room at what was then The
Gaumont, and is now
The Mayflower Theatre,
Southampton.

The transformation
process
Southampton, 1985

Gradually the group of
schoolboys takes on its
fairy guise.

Waiting
Southampton, 1985

A quiet, reflective
moment in the dressing
room before donning
full costume for
another performance of
The Dream.

The making-up of a fairy
Southampton, 1985

(Left) No member of TBC has more performances of *The Dream* to his credit than Andrew Leach. Here he finds time to photograph his friends before
(below left) taking his turn in the make-up room and
(below) having his wig carefully fitted.

Do me up at the back
Southampton, 1985

Back in the dressing room, a fellow fairy helps Andrew with the final touches to his costume.

having deposited their bags and blazers, the boys troop off across the grounds to a rehearsal room, where David puts them through their vocal paces in preparation for their performance.

Then it's back to the dressing rooms, where Tuppence distributes their urchin costumes, disappearing discreetly while they change to reappear with the squash and home-baked cake which is her hallmark. The boys set about tidying the mess of discarded clothing while the 'boss urchin' – the boy chosen as leader of this particular choir – sets about taking food orders. This is one time when I am not ignored. Tuppence repatriates the odd lost sock.

Since Carmen's urchins need to be brown-skinned, dark-haired vagrants, the blond boys disappear to the wig room while the others set about daubing themselves and each other in gravy-like make-up. Shortly, the transformation from uniformly tidy schoolboys to dishevelled and dirty urchins is complete. From this point on they are confined to the backstage area, since it is a strict rule that, other than on stage, they must not be seen in costume by the audience – the spell the opera weaves must not be broken.

There is little time to rest. The boys are gathered to the Green Room with the chorus for a warm-up led by the conductor or Chorus Master – a final opportunity to concentrate on any areas which can be honed to further perfection.

It is now early evening and the boys swarm to the Courtyard Cafe, the *al fresco*

feeding place for cast, orchestra and stage crew – where the food supplied never quite tallies with the recollection of the demands placed. David negotiates with the cafe staff, who patiently redress the perceived imbalances.

It is still an hour or so before the curtain is due to go up. As members of the audience are staking their claims to picnic areas by depositing hampers, the boys file – less exuberantly now – back to the dressing rooms. As we pass through the corridors, the powerful sounds of the Principals exercising their vocal chords periodically assail the ear from all directions. The slightly quieter atmosphere that ensues in the boys' dressing rooms may be a sign of some tension creeping in, but looking around as they settle down to homework and huddled conversations, I see nothing to suggest that this is anything other than a normal day's work.

Soon the dressing room loudspeaker's messages turn from stage crew summonses to countdown warnings. We hear the orchestra warming up and the respectful applause as the conductor takes his position. A moment's expectant silence and the overture starts.

From this point until the interval is a blur of instant impressions. Watching the conductor on the monitor at the side of the stage, his gestures followed in perfect synchronisation by the sub-conductor guiding the actors who are looking into the wings. The swirling music beating out familiar themes. The boys, high on adrenalin, awaiting their first raucous entrance. The energetic,

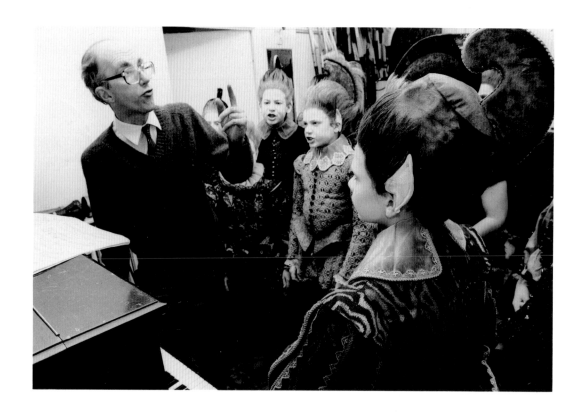

Warm-up sequence
Southampton, 1985

A study in expressions as David conducts the vocal warm-up in the conductor's dressing room – housing the only available piano at the time.

Making-up for *Carmen*
Glyndebourne, 1987

For once, the normal Glyndebourne dressing rooms could not cope with the whole of the cast, so the boys in *Carmen* were housed in temporary dressing rooms outside the main building. Also unusual was the fact that they were responsible for their own (relatively simple) make-up.

In pensive mood
Glyndebourne, 1987

As the time approaches for the curtain to go up, a quieter mood
settles upon the boys as they build their concentration for the
performance.

Gone fishin'
Glyndebourne, 1987

During rehearsals for *Carmen*, the boys get some time to relax. These two, camouflaged by their urchin make-up, take the opportunity to reel in a tiddler from the lake at Glyndebourne.

There's no escaping homework
Glyndebourne, 1987

A less favoured way of passing the time during rehearsals is homework. Even in urchin make-up, with music in the ears, and amid the splendour of Glyndebourne, it's still homework.

disciplined stagehands manipulating unwieldy scenery preparing for set changes. Soaring arias. The agonising over imperceptible imperfections. The enthusiastic applause as the curtain announces the interval.

After the lengthy intermission, with the boys anything but subdued, the second half proceeds in much the same impressionistic manner. One image that remains vivid in my memory is the stage exit of José at the tragic conclusion of the opera. The image of physical and emotional exhaustion etched on his sweat-drenched face as he reached the wings crystallised the reality of the operatic illusion in one fleeting moment. As he slumped, gasping for breath, onto the shoulder of an awaiting assistant, I genuinely feared for his survival. No distressed athlete at the end of a marathon has ever looked so totally drained. It was for me both a shocking and exhilarating moment. By the time he had been revived with the ready carafe of water – half drunk, half poured over his head – it was his turn to take a bow. A rapturous swell of cheers and applause, echoed both by the rest of the cast and those waiting in the wings, marked the audience's admiration of his skill and endeavour.

No sooner have I absorbed this spectacle and the race is on for the dressing rooms. Costumes are flung aside as a frenzy of soap and water starts the urchins' conversion back to schoolboys. Tuppence patiently collects and checks props as David sees that backs are scrubbed and dawdlers are vigorously prompted to action. As uniforms become more prevalent, the scrabble for mislaid ties and shoes subsides. Costumes, more or less neatly arranged on their appointed hangers, are handed back to the safe-keeping of Tuppence.

When all are ready, a final check that nothing is left behind, farewells to Tuppence, and David sets off for the coach at rapid pace, straggling behind him a trail of smart-looking schoolboys. They briefly acknowledge the congratulations of departing members of the audience before receiving in good spirit the assault of the awaiting company's growing impatience.

Back on the train and to awaiting parents and bed, ready for the next morning's school, where the achievements of the previous day pale into insignificance against the demands of the next chemistry test.

The real thing
Southampton, 1985

A huddle of fairies
Royal Opera House, Covent Garden, 1986

Studying some photographs from an earlier performance.

Finishing touches
Carmen, *Glyndebourne, 1987*

Putting the finishing touches to make-up amid the bustle of the
Glyndebourne dressing room.

Tuppence's cake

Carmen, *Glyndebourne, 1987*

'Tuppence' – Glyndebourne 'dresser' to the boys on frequent
occasions – distributes her famed home-baked cake.

A quiet corner
The Green Room,
Glyndebourne, 1987

The boys are expected to
keep up with their
schoolwork, although it's
not always completed in
the elegant surroundings of
Glyndebourne's Green
Room – more normally
associated with warm-ups
before the performance.
And the reading matter is
not always for school.

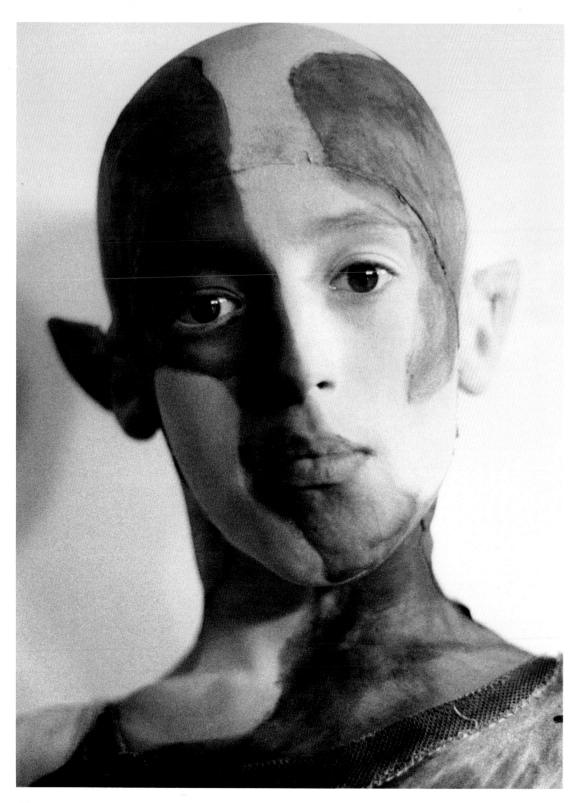

Ominous fairy
Royal Opera House, 1986

Piers Carr in full costume
and make-up for the
Sadlers Wells production
of *The Dream*.

Fairy circle

Royal Opera House, Covent Garden 1986

David Squibb takes a vocal warm-up, surrounded by the elemental
fairies of the Sadlers Wells production.

Winged warm-up

Glyndebourne, 1989

Conductor Jane Glover takes the final warm-up for the boys.

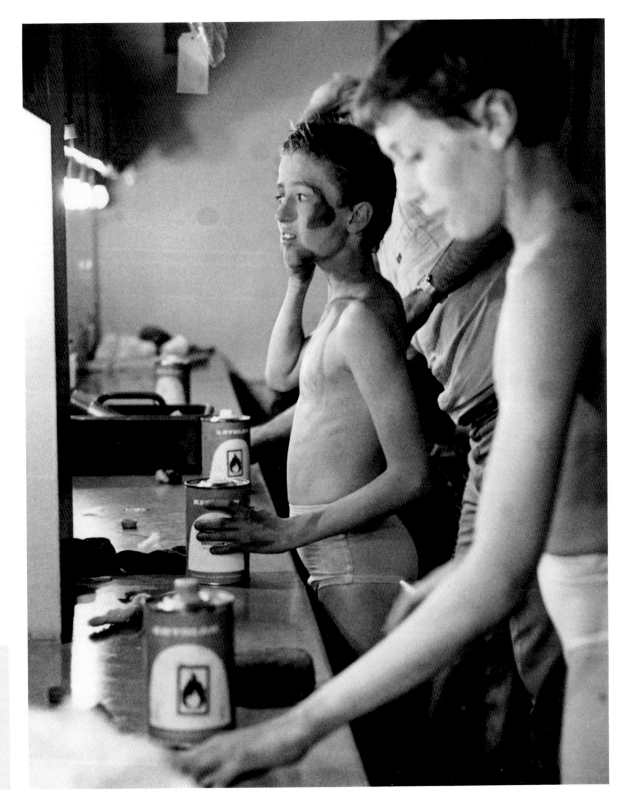

End of play
Covent Garden, 1986

After the final curtain, the gradual transformation back to schoolboys begins.

Recipe for an urchin
Carmen, *Glyndebourne, 1987*

(Left)
First catch your choirboy...
Paul Middleton outside the Glyndebourne stage door before preparing for his part.

(Below left)
...add costume and a wig...

(Right)
...and some make-up.

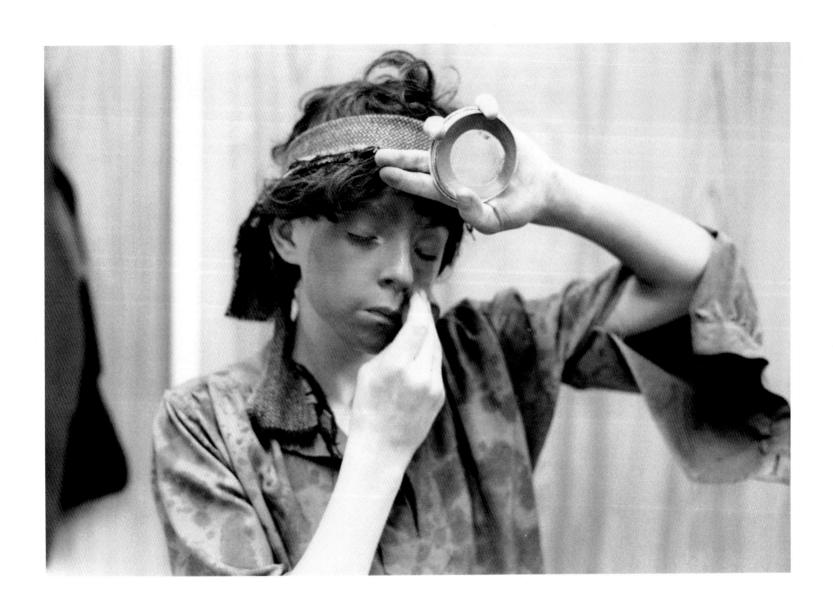

The final result
Carmen,
Glyndebourne, 1987

Paul Middleton – now
the complete urchin –
ready to take to the
stage.

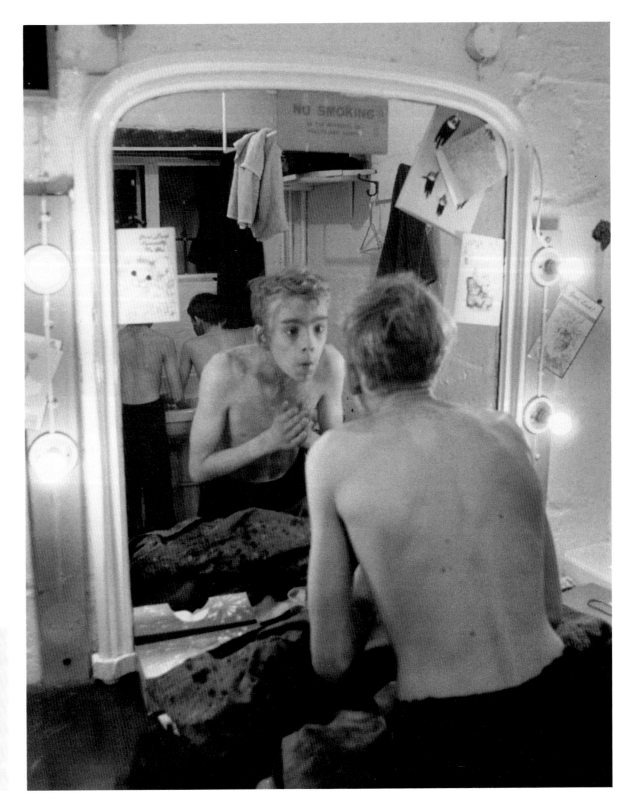

Is that really me?
Carmen,
Glyndebourne, 1987

After the performance,
Paul checks, with
some uncertainty, on
the clean-up process.

Berlioz *Te Deum*
Royal Albert Hall, 1990

TBC at the centre of the massed choirs for the rehearsal of the
Henry Wood Promenade Concert.

6   In performance

I admit to feeling something of a fraud talking about the Choir's performances. I believe it is unfair on the boys and the other performers, even when the director or management would permit it, to photograph while a public performance is in progress. So my stage photographs are usually confined to dress rehearsals and photo-calls. Even though I have worked with the Choir on countless occasions, whether recordings, concerts, operas or recitals, I have never been in the audience for a complete public performance. Indeed, my musical taste is such that I would be completely incompetent to pass any judgement on their abilities in any case. However, it would seem slightly strange to complete a book on the Choir without showing some photographs of them in performance, albeit rehearsals and recordings.

The range of work the Choir is involved in is impressive, both musically and from a photographic viewpoint. While concerts involve large numbers of boys, TV and recording studios offer the fascination of sophisticated equipment, and church settings lend a natural majesty, it is opera which provides the greatest variety of musical and photographic opportunities.

The opera with which the Choir is most readily associated is Benjamin Britten's *A Midsummer Night's Dream*. The Choir has now been featured in three different professional productions, not counting tours and revivals, amassing some 80 public performances in total, which have by coincidence, involved 80 different boys. Like all good stories, this association has more than its fair share of chance and coincidence. It started in the late 1970s when some of the boys were involved in a production of Shakespeare's play at the Churchill Theatre, Bromley.

At the same time, John Shepherd, a member of David's music teaching team at Trinity, was also in charge of the junior choir at the Royal Academy of Music. The senior students at the Academy were about to stage *The Dream*, and John was to provide the fairy chorus. Feeling that the Academy's junior choir at that time was not in a position to take these roles, John arranged with David for boys from TBC to cover the chorus parts.

As luck would have it, the conductor for the Academy production was Steuart Bedford, a contemporary of David from his own days at the Academy. By coincidence, Steuart was also preparing a production of *The Dream* for the Aldeburgh Festival, and had not at that time cast the fairies. Impressed by the boys' performance at the Academy, it

Christmas lunchtime concert
Fairfield Hall, Croydon, 1987

The annual Christmas concert at the nearest major venue to the
School is a popular part of the festive season's programme.

Christmas concert
Fairfield Hall, 1982

The diminutive choirboy
peering over his music
folder is, in fact, Tom
Squibb – one of David's
three sons to attend the
School. Tom, at 22, is
now a considerably
taller policeman.

was natural to extend the relationship to Aldeburgh, which began the Choir's professional connection with the opera.

The next coincidence was that Glyndebourne had scheduled a new production by Sir Peter Hall for the next year. Following the critical acclaim of the Aldeburgh production, the boys auditioned successfully for the new version. When Christopher Renshaw revived the Aldeburgh *Dream* at the Royal Opera House, his previous work with TBC and the Choir's involvement in the original production, again made the Trinity boys the natural choice. Finally, following the Trinity boys' performance in the 1989 Glyndebourne production, Opera London approached TBC for David Meyer's new production at Sadlers Wells and the subsequent recording. The Choir was by no means typecast, since each of the productions has featured quite different interpretations of the fairies, from the Elizabethan finery of the Glyndebourne production to the elemental imagery of Covent Garden and the Sadlers Wells primitives.

It would be wrong to take the apparent blasé attitude of the boys at face value. "It is not uncommon," says David Squibb, "for the boys to say goodbye to Glyndebourne after what they realise will be their last performance. They may present it as a bit of a joke, but you can tell they are serious underneath. It really does mean something special to them."

This insight inevitably raised in my mind the question of the boys' voices breaking – a question which I could tell was more than familiar to David. "I prefer to say 'changing' rather than breaking. Eleven- and twelve-year old boys are usually living for the day, their singing abilities are improving, and so they don't worry about their voices changing. Usually around 13, they start to find they can't quite do what they had been taking for granted. Then a marvellous thing happens – you can see them using all their experience to compensate for the change in their voices. They know when to sing out and when to keep quieter. It's a bit like an experienced older tennis player using all his skill and experience to run a far fitter, younger player off the court.

"Boys at that age tend to be much more interested in health and strength in any case. Simply, they want to grow up – to become men. So, although there is some disappointment as their life as a treble comes to an end, there are plenty of new and exciting things happening to them to compensate. Those who are particularly keen on music tend to transfer more of their interest to instrumental work.

"I don't hold with this nonsense that boys should stop singing for two years when their voices change. The chances are they would lose their singing skills altogether. It's sensible for them to cut down on their singing and it's important not to strain their voices up or down. It's easier for the church choristers because they can take on other voice parts and it's sometimes possible to use the older boys in children's operas. I think it's completely wrong for them to be told to stop singing altogether. But obviously, from a professional point of view, a boy tenor – however good – is never going to make the grade against an experienced adult."

Whilst in philosophical mood, David throws in another heart-felt view: "Compared to 20 or 30 years ago, there are now far fewer boys regularly singing in choirs throughout this country. This is a great shame because our tradition is envied by other countries – indeed, many have tried to emulate it. The enormous decrease in the number of boys in choirs has made some of us increasingly concerned for the whole future of the choral scene in Britain. Where are the tenors and basses of the future going to come from?"

The final question to David – is there a 'Trinity sound'? – brings a wry smile. "People tell me there is, although it's not something we consciously aim for. They say there's a different character about the boys' singing. I like to think that comes from the very wide range of work we do. It may also have something to do with the fact that the boys don't come here until they're 10 or 11, whilst the cathedral choir schools get their boys a couple of years earlier. So we have to develop standards very quickly.

"Sometimes I'm told we sing too dramatically for church music or too nicely for secular music: maybe that means we've got it about right."

Christmas carols
Whitgift Almshouses, Croydon, 1982

Probably the smallest audience for any of the Choir's 'performances' is at the annual carol singing for the old folk in the Almshouses which, like Trinity School itself, are a part of the Whitgift Foundation. By tradition, the boys take turns to conduct successive carols, while David Squibb gets a chance to sing.

Promenade concert

Royal Albert Hall, 1990

Conductor Gennady Rozhdestvensky rehearses the boys as part of the massed choirs in the Berlioz *Te Deum* for the 1990 BBC Proms performance. The concert was broadcast live on Radio 3.

A break in rehearsal
Royal Albert Hall, 1990

There is always plenty to talk about during any break in rehearsal.
The boys did not really realise how prestigious the occasion was
until they saw the queues outside, complete with ticket touts.

Berlioz *Te Deum*
Royal Albert Hall, 1990

Major concerts often provide the opportunity to involve large
numbers of boys – frequently 50 or more, as here, and occasionally
over 100.

(Right)
Carmina Burana
The Barbican, 1990

The boys are by no means
always centre stage.
Limited space for major
performances sometimes
forces them into a corner.

Recording the soundtrack for *Lord of the Flies*
Angel Studios, London, 1989

The Choir has been featured on the soundtracks of a number of
acclaimed films, including *Another Country*, *Highlander* and
Walkabout. This shot, taken from the production box, shows the
monitors which are used whilst synchronising the music perfectly to
the picture, often requiring minute modifications to the written score.
A memorable moment here was the look of dumb amazement when
the producer's voice came over the loudspeaker in the studio: "We
need another 28 seconds of lahs at the end of that bit". Because of
the censor's '15' rating for *Lord of the Flies*, the boys cannot yet
(legitimately, anyway) view the film to hear their performance.

Following in famous footsteps
Soundtrack recording for the film, American Friends, *Abbey Road Studios, London, 1990*

Following The Beatles' *Abbey Road* album, and the famous cover photograph which sparked so much conjecture, this must be the best known recording studio in the world. This brief recording session (and, indeed, this photograph) may not provoke quite the same degree of international interest, but will certainly be memorable for 15 young boys and one rather older photographer (who did make sure to walk across that zebra crossing!).

The Piper of Hamelin

Rehearsal for John Rutter's children's opera at Fairfield Hall, Croydon, 1981

Children's operas are another popular part of the Choir's repertoire, involving large numbers of boys, giving an opportunity to some of the older boys to continue their involvement in singing on stage, and providing the School's many instrumentalists a public platform.

Dancing to the piper's tune
Fairfield Hall, 1981

Another of my favourite photographs, simply because the scene is so perplexing. In my portfolio, I have entitled the shot, 'Orchestrated dance for select audience and two pipes', whilst the photograph also appeared in the School's magazine purporting to be an SAS training exercise. In fact, the photograph shows the Hamelin dignitaries watching as the Pied Piper clears the town of its rats.

Flight of fancy
Glyndebourne, 1987

During the television recording of the Glyndebourne production of
Ravel's *L'Enfant et les Sortilèges* for BBC Television.

Building castles in Glyndebourne
L'Enfant et les Sortilèges, *Glyndebourne, 1987*

As the TBC attendants open the storybook, the fairy-tale Princess steps out of the pop-up castle.

Hughie
Aldeburgh Festival, 1989

Matthew Kitteridge in the part of Hughie, one of the twins, in Benjamin Britten's children's opera, *The Little Sweep*.

Jamie Adams as *The Little Sweep*
The Jubilee Hall, Aldeburgh Festival, 1989

A Thames TV recording of this charming children's opera, featuring Jamie and other boys from TBC, was screened on Christmas Day 1989. This subsequent stage version was timed 40 years after its Aldeburgh premiere, at the same venue and under the direction of Basil Coleman, one of the directors of the first staging of the opera.

7   *The last word*

This book has tended to deal with the Choir from the School's perspective and from my personal view as the 'official photographer'. The last words should be from the boys themselves. I chatted with three boys at different stages of their TBC 'careers' to get their impressions of what the Choir means to them. They had much in common: articulate, confident, keenly interested in pop music and intent on careers, like law and medicine, that are far removed from the world of professional music.

Stephen Catling, aged 11 when we talked, was relatively new to the Choir, but had already undertaken a number of professional performances, including the Glyndebourne *Dream* as a soloist, Christmas concerts at The Barbican and Fairfield Hall and the recording of the soundtrack for *Lord of the Flies* at Angel Studios. "I don't think it's anything unusual because of the music standard here," he tells me.

He found *The Dream* the most difficult role so far: "It was the first time I had to do singing as well as acting and playing the recorder. I didn't really expect to have drama lessons. Remembering stage directions and hitting exact positions at the right time was quite difficult. Also the wig made me lose my sense of height at first – I kept bumping into things."

His first cathedral course at Exeter made quite an impression, with ready memories of stink bombs in the dormitory and water fights in the fields. "It was great fun and the music was quite an experience. Being away with so many friends and having so much to do made me completely forget about home most of the time."

Stephen made quite an impression himself recently. Towards the end of a rehearsal, David was suddenly surprised to see him dressed only in swimming trunks. He explained, in a matter of fact way, that he was getting ready for his race in an inter-school swimming competition that was already under way in the nearby school pool.

"It's competitive in some ways. I was a bit disappointed when I failed the audition for *The Little Sweep*. I think some of my friends are jealous of me being able to miss some afternoon lessons, but they make up for it with jokes about me being a fairy."

For the future with the Choir? "I'd like to do something on television, but who knows? You just have to see what comes along. I think when my voice breaks, that will just be the start of a new singing career – you just do your best with what you've got."

At 13, Christopher Skillicorn is a seasoned professional, coming towards the end of his boy treble days. Those days had included, at the time we talked, three different Glyndebourne productions, three cathedral courses, and a host of recitals, recordings and concerts.

He admits to finding Trinity quite daunting at first, needing two voice tests before he was accepted for the Choir. "I was very nervous before my first public performance, but afterwards it felt good. It was exciting. It's a great feeling when a performance goes well."

Despite memories of moments like dropping a stick in *Carmen* and notes 'going off', his enthusiasm shows he has clearly enjoyed his time in the Choir. "It's been very enjoyable. Quite an experience. I think it's made me less nervous. It was a bit frantic trying to fit everything in at first. But you get used to it. Christmas is always difficult because of clashes with other activities, but there's no problem keeping up with school work."

Andrew Sinclair, at 17, had his fair share of musical disappointments before achieving distinction within TBC: failing his church choir audition at the first attempt and being rejected for the Royal School of Church Music. But he was chosen to sing a solo at Croydon Parish Church at the age of 10 "because no-one else was any good".

He is one of the few remaining boys in the school who was involved in the performances of the Glyndebourne production of *The Dream* at the 1986

Hong Kong Arts Festival – the first Glyndebourne visit to Asia. "It seemed like we didn't ever go to sleep. There were 28 floors in the hotel and we'd be running up and down chasing each other and trying to avoid Mr Squibb."

He recalls that they didn't always succeed in the latter objective. "You always know the limits. If you're careful, you can get away with murder – well almost. But you can tell from his tone when he means it, and then you'd better watch out."

One of the highlights of Andrew's career has to be his appearance in the 1987 election night broadcast of *Spitting Image*, singing the haunting *Tomorrow belongs to me*, accompanied by the grotesque Cabinet puppets. "I did the rehearsal without knowing what the song was for. I couldn't believe it when they told me I was going to be on *Spitting Image*. It was especially good because I could have my hair dyed, although my parents weren't too keen. At the end, when I was supposed to be crying with emotion, they kept putting drops in my eyes and water was streaming down my face. It was strange the next day to be recognised by people in the street. In school, we watched the video in class and they kept playing it back. That was really embarrassing.

"You get used to people taking the mickey – particularly about being a fairy in *The Dream*. I don't mind if they say it to your face. I was still a treble in the fourth year, so I had a high-pitched voice when all the others had changed. I got quite a bit of leg-pulling for that.

(Right)
Christopher Skillicorn
Angel Studios, 1989

Christopher (right) during the recording of the soundtrack for *Lord of the Flies.*

"Now my voice has changed, I particularly miss Glyndebourne. That was special. I have to admit it hurts a bit when I see the youngsters going off for the train and I'm left back here. Yes, Glyndebourne was really good."

Andrew is an excellent advertisement for the Trinity all-rounder. A talented academic student, wing forward and captain of the 1st XV, and a school hockey player and swimmer, he has recently been made School Captain. He remains a keen singer – but these days as a tenor.

He is also big enough to admit to being very homesick on his first cathedral course, but is pleased now that he weathered that crisis. "I've got a lot out of being in the Choir. I think it helps you grow up more quickly. You feel comfortable talking to your parents' friends, for example. You don't always appreciate it at the time, but it's been great."

(Left)
Andrew Sinclair
Glyndebourne, 1987

Andrew in his role as an urchin in the Glyndebourne production of *Carmen*.

Printed by Jevons Brown